Circles of Love

DR R. BRASCH

Angus&Robertson
An imprint of HarperCollins*Publishers*

dedication

To my wife

Our love for each other is as unending as the lines of the

wedding ring I put on your finger so many years ago.

Our ever-renewed concern for one another and our

sharing of everything makes every day of our lives

so meaningful and fulfilling.

contents

introduction 6

the engagement ring 10

why a diamond? 15

the wedding ring 20

where the wedding ring is worn 29

removal or loss 33

stories of special rings 34

the claddagh ring 36

the turkish puzzle ring 44

the mizpah ring 47

the jewish wedding ring 51

the russian wedding ring 55

the eternity ring 58

introduction

rRings have existed since the third millennium BC in almost all cultures. They were worn AROUND or through many parts of the body. There were finger rings, TOE RINGS, nose rings, armlets and bangles. They were made from all kinds of materials, from straw and wire to platinum, silver and GOLD. Most were simple single bands while others were BEJEWELLED. Some rings were decorated with telling features, such as clasped hands, a HEART, a skull or initials. On occasion, they were engraved with enigmatic words or a message. Instead of being just ONE CIRCULAR BAND, a ring could also be a combination of several hoops — at times up to seven — joined in a diversity of ways.

Rings were chosen to serve a variety of purposes. They could express friendship, love or sorrow, the promise of marriage or an INSEPARABLE UNION. Apart from being merely symbolic, rings also fulfilled a utilitarian function. Thus, SIGNET RINGS were used from earliest times to authenticate documents with a seal. SCARAB RINGS were believed to have supernatural powers and to be able to protect their wearer against threats of the evil eye or other nefarious, invisible forces. A husband's jealousy and mistrust in a wife's FIDELITY led to the creation of yet another type of ring, ingeniously designed to ensure her FAITHFULNESS...!

Rings have indeed played a significant role in human RELATIONSHIPS and they are part of our social history, with many a RING having an intriguing story. To explore their background and learn about their TRADITIONAL MESSAGES presents a fascinating pursuit.

INTRODUCTION

& # the engagement ring

Legend tells us that the DIAMOND'S sparkle originated in a magician's spell for 'FIRES OF LOVE'. This, above all, made it the most fitting choice to adorn an ENGAGEMENT RING. It was a promise of the couple's enduring LOVE and an assurance that their married life would SPARKLE with happiness, just as the brilliant stone did. This is the origin of the sentiments expressed in the 'DIAMOND' wedding anniversary.

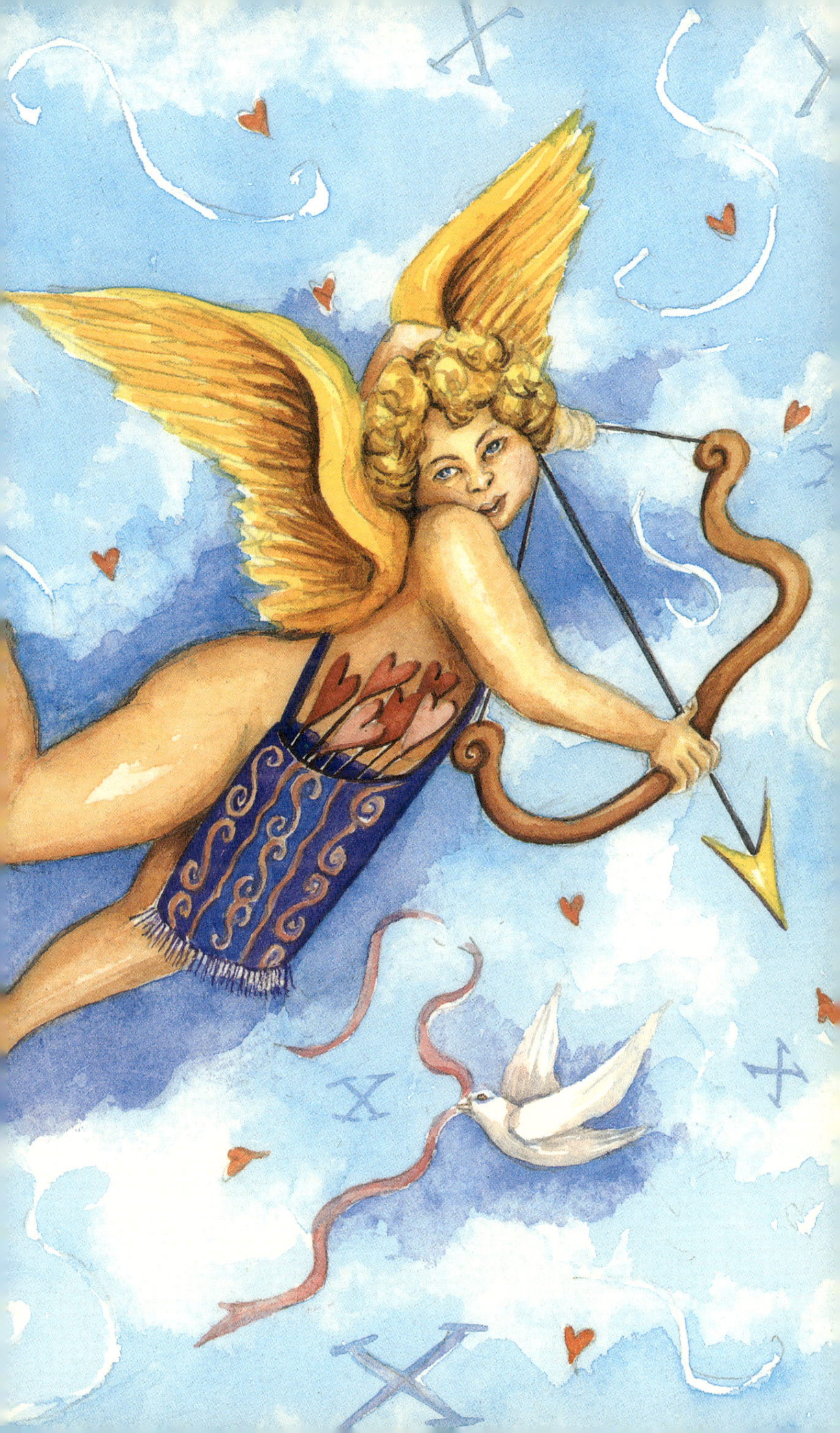

The presentation of an ENGAGEMENT RING is a romantic occasion, full of joy and promise. Paradoxically, however, its original use in ANCIENT ROMAN SOCIETY, from where it spread to other parts of the world, was as a legally binding commercial transaction. The engagement ring was not only a token of BETROTHAL, it was also a secular PLEDGE to confirm the arrangement of the future marriage. Conspicuously displayed for all to see, it meant that the girl had been 'ACQUIRED' and was no longer 'available'.

The custom was also a survival of the general practice in early cultures to ratify a deal by a CONTRACT which had to be signed by both parties. This they did by means of a SIGNET ring, impressing its seal on the relevant document; in ancient Mesopotamia, for instance, this was a clay tablet with CUNEIFORM characters.

To start with, Roman law restricted the use of GOLDEN rings to the privileged upper class, senators and magistrates. Ordinary people had to be satisfied with a simple iron hoop devoid of any kind of ornamentation, and certainly without a JEWEL. The PASSAGE OF TIME, however, altered circumstances. When the empire became more affluent and wealth spread to other members of the community, LOVE was able to overrule law and the original humiliating prohibition was forgotten. Those who could afford it replaced their IRON RING with one made from GOLD or some other precious metal. Frequently, the band was adorned with a telling motif, such as a LOVERS' KNOT or clasped hands. Not least, it was enriched by some gem or even a combination of precious stones.

why a diamond?

Traditionally, a diamond adorns the engagement ring. History claims that, in 1477, Emperor Maximilian I of Austria was one of the first to give a DIAMOND RING to his fiancée, Mary of Burgundy. The choice of a DIAMOND was not just due to its intrinsic value or conspicuousness, it was also based on a combination of long-held beliefs.

THE ENGAGEMENT RING

In earlier, more SUPERSTITIOUS TIMES, people imagined that invisible malevolent forces continually tried to destroy human HAPPINESS. No doubt a couple engaged to be married would be a prime target. It was further assumed that those evil spirits, belonging to the world of darkness, would shun light, therefore anything bright would scare them off. This made a diamond in a ring the perfect safeguard, its REFLECTED LIGHT warding off any devilish forces near by. Thus the couple's love would no longer be threatened and nothing would break their ENGAGEMENT.

Another, even more fanciful assumption which was once prevalent was that the diamond possessed PROCREATIVE POWER! For instance, it was widely held that two stones set in one ring would multiply. And, by association, some of the diamond's supposed SEXUAL POTENCY would be transferred to the wearer. The presentation of a DIAMOND to one's fiancée, therefore, had a very practical meaning and purpose, as well as a SYMBOLIC one. To be effective, it was further believed the stone had to be set unbacked, so that it was able to touch the skin.

The diamond was known to be one of the world's hardest substances, which no other STONE could cut or scratch. It was therefore also imagined to give CONSTANCY and permanence to the forthcoming marital union. Its transparency made the diamond a symbol of purity, innocence and SINCERITY. Apart from indicating the wearer's virtue, it also expressed the PLEDGE on the part of both the man and the woman never to deceive each other.

The Italians used to call the diamond 'the stone of RECONCILIATION'. They were convinced that if a disagreement ever threatened a couple's happiness, a diamond would MAGICALLY restore harmony. Hence its presence in a ring ensured a lasting and happy relationship between husband and wife.

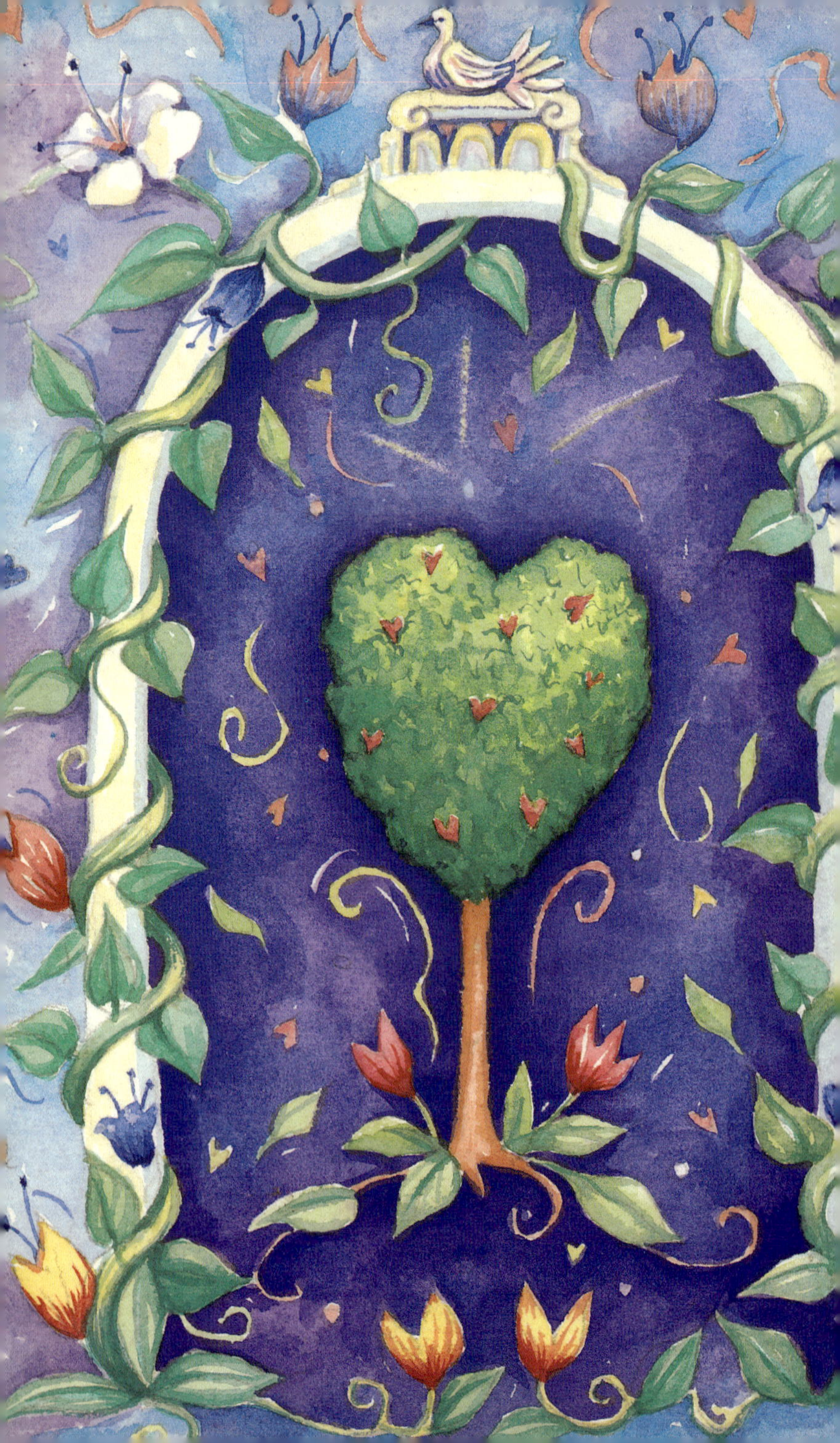

the wedding ring

In early times, the presentation of a WEDDING RING signified the transfer of authority as much as the JOINING of two people. By placing the ring on his BRIDE'S finger, the man publicly endowed her with all his rights and she became the MISTRESS of his house.

The WEDDING BAND developed out of the betrothal ring. However, its story goes back much further, to the very beginning of the institution of marriage. Far removed from the beautiful SYMBOLISM it has today, in its original form a ring served a variety of totally different functions.

One of them was part of primitive man's customary means of acquiring a wife: he simply CAPTURED a woman. To secure his precious booty and prevent her from escaping whilst carrying her home, he ENCIRCLED both her wrists and her ankles with fetters!

1

Less crude was the alternative method of purchasing a wife. In this case the ring was not a gift, but represented the PRICE he had paid to her family, the original owners. Having safely brought his CONQUEST (or purchase) home, the man was naturally concerned about keeping and protecting his VALUABLE asset. After all, the woman might still try to run away; or, even if she had settled down as a LOYAL wife, she might be harmed or harassed by evil spirits, jealous of the couple's newly found MARITAL BLISS. Early man was convinced only magic could prevent either from happening, so he bound a rope around his bride's body. This 'MAGIC CIRCLE' would, he thought, not only protect her by repelling outside attacks, but it would fetter her to him in spirit, too, thus making their souls mingle.

As society became more civilised, these practices were discarded and the large 'CIRCLE', as it were, contracted to the size of a modern ring. However, it still retained much of its imagined magical potency.

It is generally assumed that, in the seventeenth century BC, the ancient EGYPTIANS were among the first to use the ring as a symbol of marriage. They placed circular bands on the fingers of those joining in MATRIMONY. According to their hieroglyphic scripts, these circles symbolised eternity: just as their lines were unending, so would be the couple's affection. Indeed, the ring would serve not merely as a constant reminder of the PERMANENCY of marriage, but as a magic means to ensure it.

Wedding rings were made from all types of MATERIAL. Those who could afford it — and by law were permitted to do so — chose GOLD. Apart from its value, gold also conveyed a meaningful SYMBOLIC message. One of the early Fathers of the Church, Tertullian (AD 160–220) spoke of gold as 'the nobler and PURER METAL'. Remaining 'longer uncorrupted', it intimated 'the generous, sincere and durable affection which ought to be between the MARRIED parties'.

THE WEDDING RING

Interestingly, Christianity rejected and condemned the wedding ring as a PAGAN accessory for several centuries. Only gradually did the Church adopt it, ultimately making it an essential part of its CONJUGAL rites and a symbol of the sanctity of marriage. Its CIRCULAR shape served to remind the couple of the harmony, perfection and UNENDING LOVE that should prevail through all the days of their married life. Ninth-century Pope Nicholas I was the first to refer to the specific Christian use of the WEDDING ring.

Though the wearing of a wedding ring is now an almost UNIVERSAL custom, the practice varies in detail. In some countries, the bride and groom EXCHANGE rings. In others, the minister, after having blessed the rings, places them on the fingers of those about to be joined in HOLY MATRIMONY. In England, it was the tradition for a long time that the bride alone would wear a ring.

THE WEDDING RING

Today, it has become the general FASHION for both parties to do so. According to German custom, the same rings that serve as a TOKEN of a couple's engagement become their wedding rings. They are simply moved from the left hand to the right.

With their initial interpretation of almost everything as having a SEXUAL connotation, early psychoanalysts saw the representation of the male organ in the finger and that of the female in the ring, which were thus JOINED together.

where the wedding ring is worn

A variety of TRADITIONS accounts for the choice of hand and the specific finger for the wearing of the wedding ring.

The selection of the third finger of the left hand has been attributed to ANCIENT faulty anatomy which taught that a vein led straight to the heart from this finger. However mistaken, it is still a BEAUTIFUL explanation. Another reason is linked with early symbolism where the right hand represented dominance and the left submission. By placing the ring on the bride's left hand, the

GROOM made her understand — without saying it in so many words — that from now on she was his PROPERTY and that he was the master of their home.

The choice of the right hand is associated with this hand's traditional use in taking an OATH. To confirm the truth of a statement, people either lifted their right hand or placed it on the Bible. Likewise, as a token of the MARRIAGE VOW, the ring belonged to this hand. Rather more poetically, the use and selection of this hand was meant to express how a WIFE was 'like a man's right hand'.

A solely utilitarian explanation is that the THIRD FINGER was the least active of the hand. A ring placed there would least inconvenience its

CIRCLES OF LOVE

wearer, and there was less likelihood of it being worn out or damaged. An equally practical consideration was the retention and SPAN of the ring finger. Whereas every other finger can be stretched independently, the third one cannot be extended to its full length on its own. This prevents a ring from easily slipping off, making the third finger the most secure safeguard for so PRECIOUS an object.

THE WEDDING RING

Nowadays, the ring is immediately put on the finger on which it is to stay at the marriage CEREMONY. However, this was not always the case. In an ancient Church ritual, still practised in the sixteenth century, the ring was systematically moved three times prior to finding its PERMANENT place. Each change was introduced or accompanied by successive parts of the TRINITARIAN formula. With the words 'In the name of the Father', the PRIEST placed the ring on the thumb. Whilst saying, 'In the name of the Son', he moved it to the forefinger and then, with 'and of the Holy Ghost', to the middle finger. With the closing word 'Amen', he slipped the RING on the third or ring finger, sealing the marriage bond.

removal or loss

The removal of her wedding ring by a bride has always been regarded as an OMINOUS SIGN. Even if it is only temporarily removed, such action was seen as a threat to the PERMANENCY of the couple's love. Worse still, should the ring be LOST or broken, it was thought a grim foreboding of the loss of MARITAL HAPPINESS.

This SUPERSTITION is based on primitive society's belief in SYMPATHETIC magic. Anything happening or done to an inanimate object would similarly affect those to whom that object belonged, or who were LINKED with it.

stories of special rings

Most cultures have created their own type of WEDDING RING, each with its specific story and MESSAGE. Still, no matter what form the rings take, or what their size, material or artistic value may be, all share the SYMBOLISM of the inseparable and unending link forged by MATRIMONY, the new reality in the lives of both bride and groom of belonging to one another.

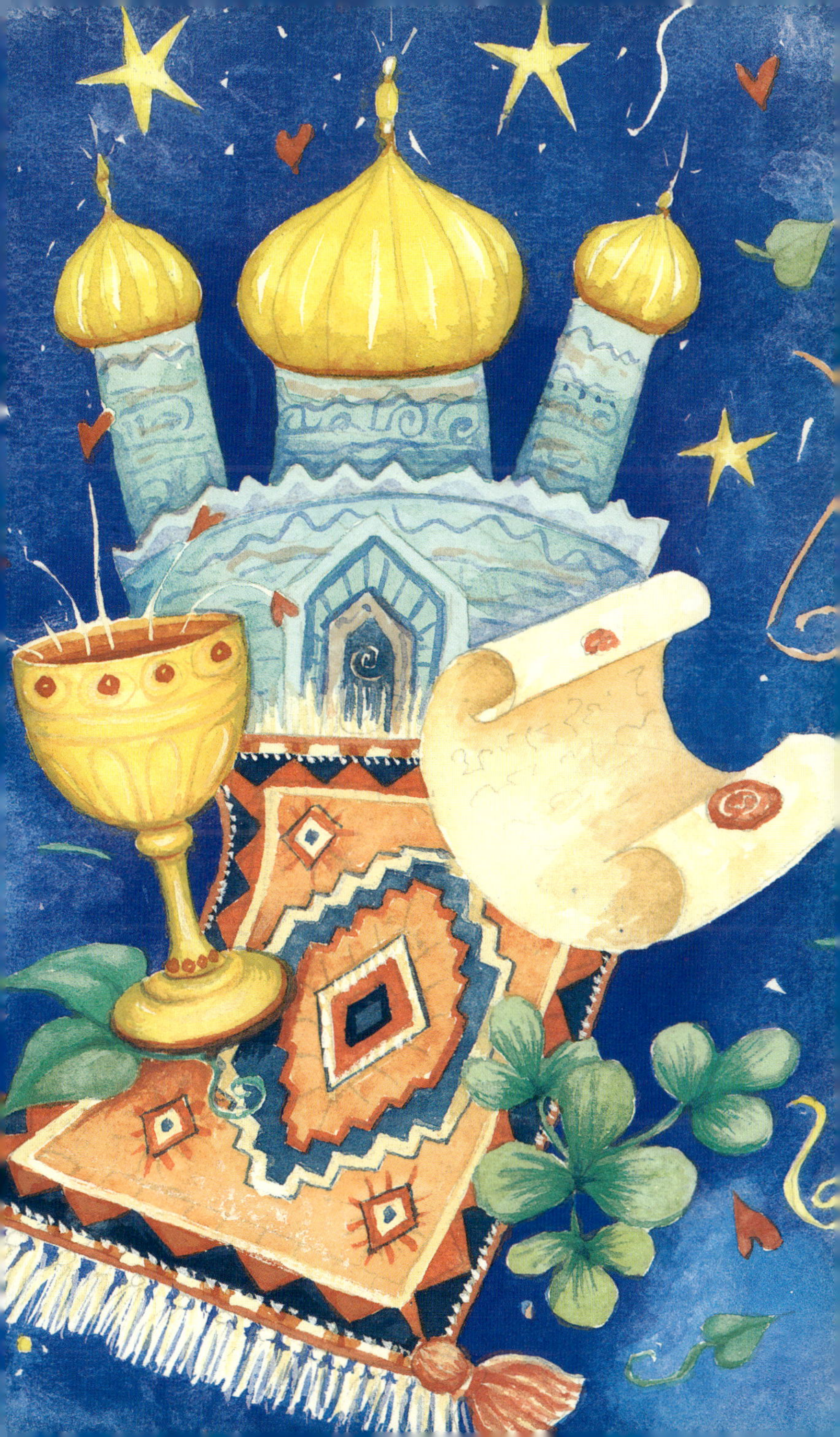

the claddagh ring

The claddagh ring, SYMBOL OF LOVE and of Ireland, is named for CLADDAGH, an Irish fishing village on Galway Bay. The word refers to the flat stony shore or beach there, known as the *claddagh* in Gaelic.

Claddagh was established in 1232, and the settlement of thatched mud houses existed until 1934. It was a closed community, its residents being very proud of their past and jealous of their INDEPENDENCE. Claddagh was always ruled by an elected head who, during the SEVEN CENTURIES of this mini-state's history, was known by a variety of titles. At times, he was referred to simply as the 'mayor' or 'the admiral' of Galway Bay, at others, more MAJESTICALLY, as 'the King'. His boat had white sails, distinct from those of all other vessels of the fishing fleet which were made from either black or brown cloth. The last ruler passed away in 1954, at 90 years of age.

STORIES OF SPECIAL RINGS

Claddagh people preferred to choose their spouses from among themselves. They were equally anxious to preserve their local CUSTOMS: One of them — and probably the most outstanding — was the wearing of the claddagh ring. Though its prototype is thought to go back to ROMAN days, Claddagh citizens made this ring their very own. Early specimens, wrought in gold, silver and bronze, are MASTERPIECES of jewellery design. They are now treasured exhibits in the National Museum of Ireland and the Victoria and Albert Museum in London.

Traditionally, the claddagh ring is shaped in the form of TWO HANDS holding a heart, which is surmounted by a crown. The heart stood for LOVE, whilst the crown expressed unswerving LOYALTY. These rings were valued heirlooms,

CIRCLES OF LOVE

and were lovingly handed down from mother to daughter. The claddagh ring served a threefold romantic purpose: as a friendship ring, an engagement ring and a WEDDING RING. Whichever of the three purposes it was chosen for was cleverly indicated by the way in which it was worn. Placed on the right hand with the crown nearest the wrist, it signified that one's heart was still to be CONQUERED.

When engaged or married, one wore the ring on the left hand. If BETROTHED, the heart was made to point towards the fingertip; turned inwards, it intimated that one was MARRIED.

Traditions differ as to the origin of the CLADDAGH RING. Though separated in time by a century, two of the most popular explanations are linked with members of the Joyce family (also spelled Ioyce), who were natives of Galway.

The earlier sixteenth-century legend claims that the first CLADDAGH RING was a well-deserved and miraculous GIFT to Margaret Joyce. Domingo de Rona, a wealthy SPANISH MERCHANT whose business brought him frequently to Galway, met Margaret on one of his visits. He FELL IN LOVE with her and she became his wife. Unfortunately, however, their happiness was short-lived. Soon after their marriage Domingo died, with Margaret inheriting his vast FORTUNE.

In 1596, Margaret remarried, her second husband being Oliver Og French, the mayor of Galway. He certainly did not wed her because of her wealth — in fact, he left the use and administration of Margaret's large LEGACY entirely up to her. She did not spend any of the money on herself. Instead, she donated it to municipal improvement, paying for the construction of numerous bridges.

One day, so the story goes, an EAGLE dropped a GOLDEN RING into her lap — the very first claddagh ring. This was regarded not just as a mere fortunate accident but as a divine reward for her SELFLESS generosity. The ring had been sent 'from on high', in every sense of the word.

STORIES OF SPECIAL RINGS

Much more down-to-earth is the second tradition. This tells us how, during the second half of the seventeenth century, Galway citizen Richard Joyce was captured by PIRATES whilst on his way to the West Indies. They sold him as a slave to a wealthy Moorish GOLDSMITH in Algiers; this goldsmith trained Richard in his craft, and he soon excelled in it.

In 1689, King William III of England SUCCEEDED in obtaining the release of all captured English subjects, including Joyce. By that time his Moorish master had grown fond of him. He implored him to stay on, promising him the hand of his daughter in marriage and half of all his POSSESSIONS. However, Joyce was not tempted. He was adamant in wanting to return to his native village in far-off Galway. He carried all the knowledge and CRAFTSMANSHIP he had acquired during his captivity with him and, not least, the very idea of the CLADDAGH RING. According to tradition, Joyce made the first of these rings as a token of his gratitude to the king to whom he owed his freedom.

Some SPECIMENS of the claddagh ring still in existence actually carry the initials 'R.I.' and have consequently been attributed to Richard. They also show an ANCHOR, which has puzzled people. One explanation is that Joyce made the first claddagh ring whilst still a slave in Africa. The anchor was, therefore, meant to SYMBOLISE how deeply he was still attached to his distant homeland and his hope that one day he would return there.

STORIES OF SPECIAL RINGS

the turkish puzzle ring

The Turkish puzzle ring has been adopted and ADMIRED in many countries. This ring is not one solid band, but is made from various parts, combining at least three bands which are cleverly INTERLOCKED. Any attempt to put them back together once they are separated presents an exacting and formidable puzzle. A PUZZLE RING may therefore be a very thoughtful gift, providing a friend with long hours of entertainment, or a group with a lively CONTEST as to who can first achieve the feat of reassembling it.

Traditionally, however, the ring was first introduced for a totally different and not so pleasant reason. It was a gift from a MISTRUSTFUL husband to his wife! If he was about to go to war or take an extended trip, and was afraid that during his absence she might get bored and be TEMPTED to yield to other men's advances, he had to find some means to keep her BUSY. What could better achieve this aim than to give her, on his departure, a disassembled PUZZLE RING? 'Puzzling out' how its parts FITTED TOGETHER would fully occupy her, theoretically leaving her no time for any other activity. On his safe return, the husband would expect to find the ring in ONE piece!

An alternative explanation is also based on this idea of a husband's determination to guard his wife's CHASTITY during any absence on his part. However, this time it was not by presenting her with the various parts of the ring, but with the COMPLETE item. He placed it on her hand and she was to keep it there till his return. If she removed it to hide her MARRIED STATUS, the ingeniously interlocked pieces would come apart and she would have great difficulty rejoining them, thus revealing her UNFAITHFULNESS. Aware of this threatened 'give-away', she would, hopefully, refrain from committing ADULTERY and the puzzle ring would have achieved its purpose as a safeguard against INFIDELITY.

the mizpah ring

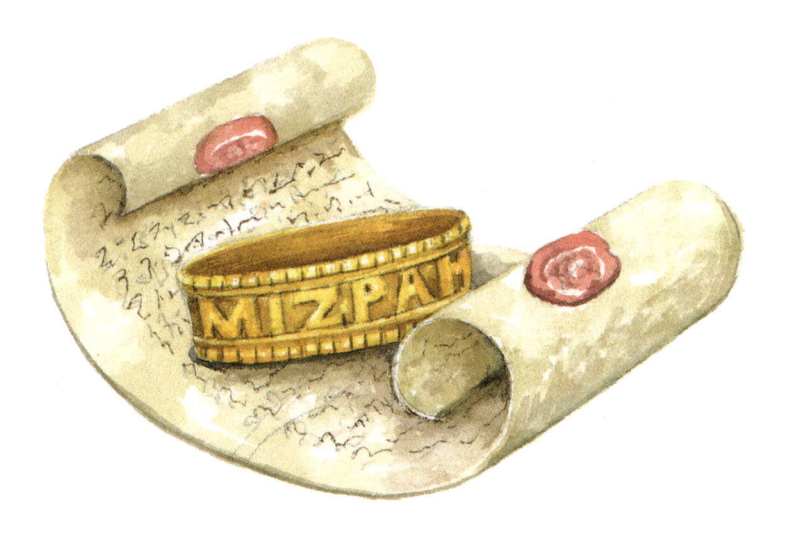

The Hebrew word *mizpah* expresses the SENTIMENT 'May the Lord watch between me and thee'. Ornaments with 'mizpah' inscribed upon them were often exchanged between LOVERS in Victorian times.

STORIES OF SPECIAL RINGS

A mizpah ring, so named for the inscription which is EMBOSSED or engraved on it, is usually chosen as a gift for someone very close who is about to go away for a long time. Its purpose was TWOFOLD. First of all, this ring was meant to ensure that even while the recipient was away, the donor's thoughts would constantly be with him or her. Simultaneously, it implored God to watch over both of them during their SEPARATION.

Mizpah is the Hebrew word for WATCH TOWER. Its present-day application to a ring is linked with the biblical account of one of the dramatic incidents in the patriarch Jacob's life. Becoming aware that his PROSPERITY had made his uncle

Laban envious, Jacob was concerned for his SAFETY and that of his family. He fled during his uncle's temporary absence, taking his wives, children and possessions with him. On his return three days later, Laban's anger was roused and he set off after Jacob, catching up with him in the hill country of GILEAD.

However, with God's intervention, what had threatened to become a hostile confrontation changed into a RECONCILIATION. Jacob and Laban made a pact, pledging never to harm or hurt one another. To commemorate the occasion and to serve as a witness to their commitment, they erected a heap of STONES at the site of their encounter.

STORIES OF SPECIAL RINGS

This cairn was to be a PERMANENT MEMORIAL of their promise and so they named it *Mizpah*, a word used both as a BENEDICTION and a warning. It summarised the words Laban then spoke: 'The Lord watch between me and you, when we are out of sight of each other.' (Gen. 31: 49)

Divorced from its context of family conflict, the message conveyed by both the uninscribed monument and Laban's words was so BEAUTIFUL that it became a popular prayer for God's 'watchfulness' over someone about to depart. 'MIZPAH' also came to express the determination of both parties to stay close together in HEART AND MIND, no matter how far apart they were, or for how long they might be absent from one another.

the jewish wedding ring

Examples of Jewish WEDDING RINGS from sixteenth and seventeenth-century Germany and Venice still exist. Often the HEBREW words *Mazal tov* – the traditional Jewish wish for 'good luck' – is either engraved or in relief around the HOOP.

Just as Christianity only adopted the WEDDING RING at a comparatively late date, so did

Judaism, in the fifth century AD. To start with, the ring simply served as a TOKEN of the groom's ability, and his pledge, to maintain a home. However, the ring soon assumed a new meaning, indicating that henceforth the husband endowed his wife with all the AUTHORITY he himself possessed.

Ultimately, the wedding ring came to symbolise the SANCTITY of the marriage bond. This role was reflected in the very formula which still accompanies the PRESENTATION of the ring: slipping it on his bride's finger, the groom proclaims, 'With this ring you are *consecrated* unto me...' in the presence of witnesses. It is a most SIGNIFICANT and very beautiful choice of words.

The Jewish wedding ring was especially cherished as a precious MEMENTO of a sacred occasion. In the past, goldsmiths embellished it in exquisite and often unique ways, creating rings of ELABORATE BEAUTY. They were ornamented with a model of a house, a synagogue or the temple in Jerusalem, all shown in INTRICATE detail with miniature windows, gabled roofs, or even a movable weather vane. The house represented the new home the couple were about to establish and their PROMISE to make it an abode of true and lasting LOVE. Equally, it was meant to stress the HIGH REGARD in which the husband held his wife, recalling the Talmudic saying that, 'A man's home is his WIFE.'

When the choice of such particular architectural DECORATION rendered a ring too cumbersome to be worn constantly, it was kept at home or at the local synagogue. In fact, it was not always a finger ring. Occasionally, its size was so EXTRAORDINARY that it was designed to serve as a holder for the BRIDE'S BOUQUET!

By way of contrast, the majority of English Jewish wedding rings were PLAIN HOOPS made from gold or other metal. Gemstones were rare, the more usual distinction being a simple HEBREW INSCRIPTION.

the russian wedding ring

Several explanations have been given for the so-called Russian wedding ring, a combination of THREE INTERTWINED RINGS, each of a different colour gold.

STORIES OF SPECIAL RINGS

It has been seen as symbolising the HOLY TRINITY, the central dogma of Christian theology which occupies a prominent place in Russian Orthodox Church rituals. The SACRAMENT of holy matrimony was solemnised in the name of the Holy Trinity, thus the triple ring would constantly remind the couple of the sanctity of their UNION.

According to a second explanation, two of the rings represented the bride and groom being joined in marriage, while the third one stood for the witness whose presence legalised their bond in PERPETUITY. Various methods were used for joining the three bands. One way was to

INTERWEAVE the rings. Alternatively, they were held together by a pair of CLASPED HANDS. This was reminiscent of the 'handfasting' custom which once was part of a betrothal, being the confirmation of the marriage AGREEMENT with a handshake.

There is also a claim that, in its present form, the Russian wedding ring was designed as late as 1923 by CARTIER, the internationally renowned jewellers. It was to be yet another of their distinctive CREATIONS, in which they adopted and made use of an ancient tradition, rendering it in their own EXQUISITE STYLE.

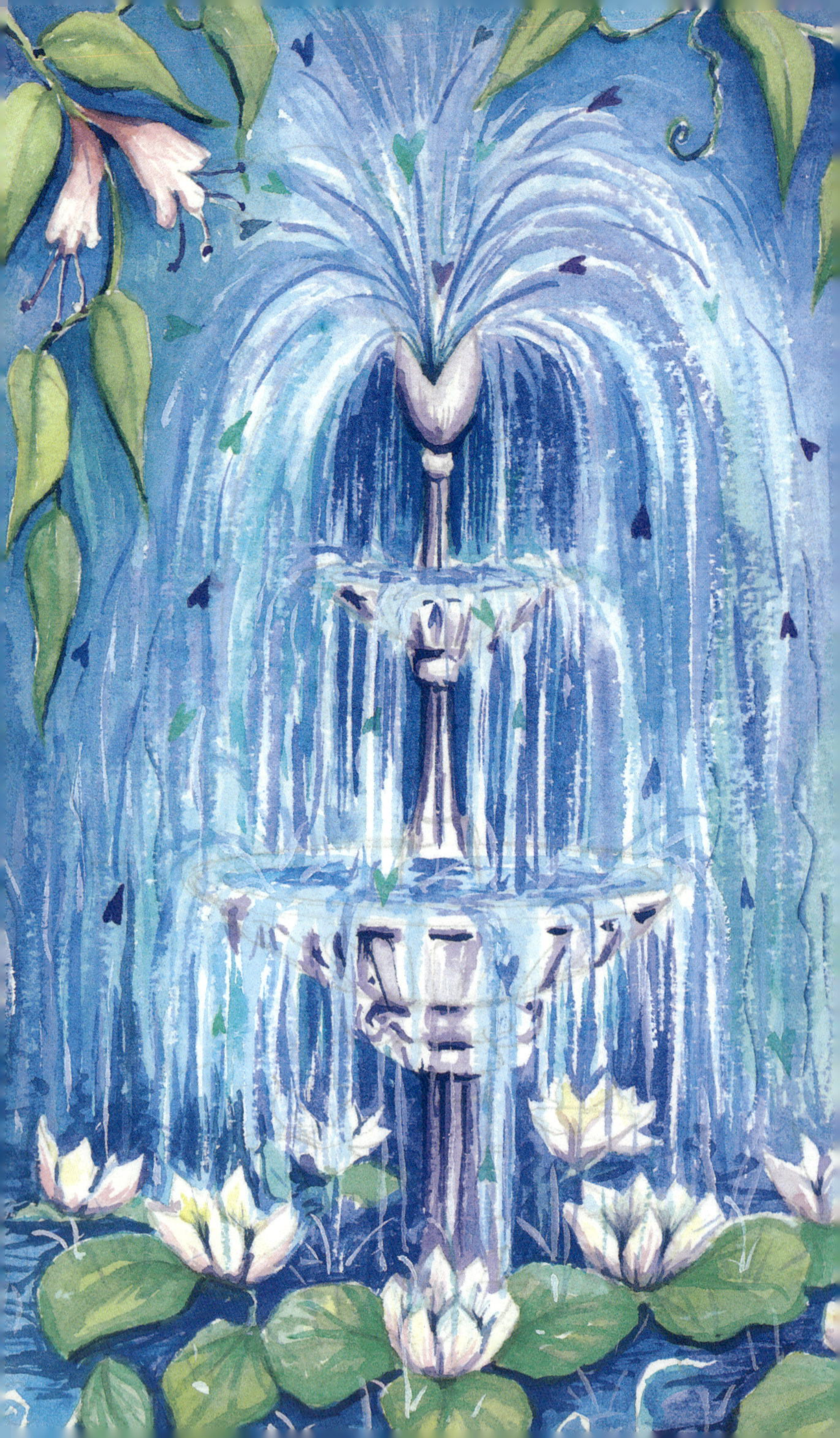

the eternity ring

One of the favourite forms of the ETERNITY RING — especially during the nineteenth century — was that of a snake, with the snake swallowing its tail: a traditional symbol of PERMANENCE. To render the ring even more precious, DIAMONDS were chosen to represent the snake's eyes and to adorn its head.

It used to be customary for a husband to present his wife with an additional ring on the occasion of their FIRST WEDDING ANNIVERSARY. It was meant to express the everlasting nature of their bond, and so was called an ETERNITY ring. More recently, it has become common to give an 'eternity ring' later on in the marriage, on the occasion of a SPECIAL anniversary; thus, they are also sometimes known as 'ANNIVERSARY rings'.

Traditionally, the eternity ring is placed on the ring finger, as the last of the now THREE bands. Usually, it is in the form of a wedding ring. However, it is not a plain hoop nor does it carry a single diamond or gemstone, like an 'engagement ring'. Instead, it is ADORNED with gemstones, often set all around it in an UNENDING CIRCLE and so symbolising the 'eternal' continuity of the couple's affection.

The eternity ring often serves as a gift on the birth of the first child – in which case 'MATERNITY RING' would probably be a more appropriate designation!

THE ETERNITY RING

All efforts have been made to contact copyright owners. Where this has not
been possible, the publishers invite the persons concerned to contact them.

Angus&Robertson
An imprint of HarperCollins*Publishers*, Australia

First published in Australia in 1996

Copyright © Rudolph Brasch 1996
Illustrations © HarperCollins*Publishers* 1996

This book is copyright.
Apart from any fair dealing for the purposes of private study, research,
criticism or review, as permitted under the Copyright Act, no part may
be reproduced by any process without written permission.
Inquiries should be addressed to the publishers.

HarperCollins*Publishers*
25 Ryde Road, Pymble, Sydney NSW 2073, Australia
31 View Road, Glenfield, Auckland 10, New Zealand
77–85 Fulham Palace Road, London W6 8JB, United Kingdom
Hazelton Lanes, 55 Avenue Road, Suite 2900, Toronto, Ontario M5R 3L2
and 1995 Markham Road, Scarborough, Ontario, M1B 5M8, Canada
10 East 53rd Street, New York NY 10022, USA

National Library of Australia Cataloguing-in-Publication data:

Brasch, R. (Rudolph), 1912–
　Circles of Love.
　ISBN 0 207 185107
　1.Rings — Folklore. 2.Betrothal — Miscellanea. 3.Marriage customs and
　rites — Miscellanea. I.Title.
391.7

Illustrations by Penny Lovelock

Printed in Hong Kong
9 8 7 6 5 4 3 2 1
00 99 98 97 96